The Volcano

BOOKS BY NORMAN DUBIE

The Volcano
The Insomniac Liar of Topo
Untitled Najaf
The Spirit Tablets at Goa Lake
Ordinary Mornings of a Coliseum
The Mercy Seat: Collected & New Poems, 1967–2001
The Amulet
The Funeral
The Clouds of Magellan
Radio Sky
Groom Falconer
The Springhouse
Selected and New Poems
The Window in the Field
The Everlastings
Odalisque in White
The City of the Olesha Fruit
A Thousand Little Things
The Illustrations
In the Dead of the Night
Popham of the New Song
Indian Summer
Prayers of the North American Martyrs
Alehouse Sonnets
The Horsehair Sofa

The Volcano

POEMS BY NORMAN DUBIE

COPPER CANYON PRESS
PORT TOWNSEND, WASHINGTON

Printed in the United States of America

Cover art: *Island,* 1994. Monoprint by Denny Moers.

Copper Canyon Press is in residence at Fort Worden State Park in Port Townsend, Washington, under the auspices of Centrum. Centrum is a gathering place for artists and creative thinkers from around the world, students of all ages and backgrounds, and audiences seeking extraordinary cultural enrichment.

LIBRARY OF CONGRESS CATALOGING-IN-PUBLICATION DATA

Dubie, Norman, 1945–
  The volcano / Norman Dubie.
    p. cm.
  ISBN 978-1-55659-326-0 (pbk. : alk. paper)
  I. Title.

PS3554.U255V65 2010
811'.54—dc22

2010022864

98765432 FIRST PRINTING

COPPER CANYON PRESS
Post Office Box 271
Port Townsend, Washington 98368
www.coppercanyonpress.org

Acknowledgments

The American Poetry Review: "The Boxcars of Mars," "The Canvas Boat," "The Ceremony," "The Fourth Generation of Summer," "In These Streets with the Binary Trees," "Pastoral," "The Siege of Horizons," "The Song of the Strangelet," and "Stockbridge Reservation"

Blackbird: "Behind the Old Soldiers' Hospital," "Cantor, Frege & Gödel," "Herman Melville's Book of Four Sentences," "Not the Bathing Tank at Madras: A Romance," and "South Boston Morning, '53"

Burnside Review: "The Grazing Higgs Bison," "Puke," and "Sasquatch"

Crazyhorse: "Again the Twentieth-Century Realism" and "The Magnesia Caesar"

The Fiddlehead: "Bureau Case Number LXXXVIII," "The Hours," "Jubilee of Surprising Agreement," "Plaquemines Parish," and "Stringy Goats of Gold Nuclei Evaporate Before My Eyes"

42opus: "The Salt Cedar Fires of '08," "2012," and "The Volcano"

Gulf Coast: "Le Monde" and "Spirit Pond"

Hayden's Ferry Review: "Desert Carousel: Missiles and Instructions," "Landmine: Field of Copper Wings," "The Sabotage of Arks," and "Sunset over Decatur, Illinois"

Interim: "The Black Canal at Bruges," "An Early Morning for Tito," "History," "In a World of Cows," and "A Nativity Canvas for My Daughter"

Lannan Foundation: "Desiccated Deer Akimbo in Barbed Wire"

The Laurel Review: "The Arbor," "In Iceland," and "Tibet"

Narrative: "The Exeter Messenger Aboard the RMS *Lusitania*," "In the Night Dulse of White Breakers a Falstaff Drops His Pike," "The Lost Adages of Maestro Pacal," "The Protestant Rye," and "Untitled"

Packingtown Review: "The Early Evening Phenomena of Winter Sabbath," "Of the Roman Gladiator's Mad Elephant," "Pontius Pilate," and "Tiresias in an Arcturus Springtime" *for my sister*

Contents

The Volcano

Desert Carousel: Missiles and Instructions

The signatures of a kerosene stove,
a small cloth pipe-organ,
squares of mica, squares of knitted asbestos,
the old wooden heads of the horses
are rouged and bent
as if in sadness over the circle
and the extravagant losses
like sardines for dollars in Fallujah.

Now on this cold October night, lonely
in the dark alkali branches, it seems
a gold standard. Robin's eggs
for a sip of chicken soup,
or the bartering of donkey shit
free of nettles for tiger shit
with the egg sacs of termites.

In the ranks of the poor my shade
follows
like a troop of mimes
folding into a shop window:
éclairs, cherry buntings,
and carrot cake of trackless snowy pasturage.

We would be sick
just trying to eat it.
Better the tiger's eggs and a few undigested bones
for the breaking.

I

42° north latitude

109° east longitude

South Boston Morning, '53:

Very pragmatic closets of falling water,
bath and sewer, complex
dwellers eating black bread,
molasses, and stringy beef,
eggs like fat flowers
smack the backs of griddlecakes
and rain is thrown against the window
white and elastic with one blue gull
in a loud commentary.

The sea is dark and choppy.
So far, out on the vellum streets
only taxis.
Three nuns sit on the stone bench
and study the storm without contempt,

without leaping into the arms of it—
though wild brides they may be,
though sea air, in heavy volume,
is pushing the dull gray farms
of New Hampshire
into a long familiar misery—
the Sisters
are their own dark umbrellas, folding
                    among the winter trees.

Behind the Old Soldiers' Hospital

Steam banks chug out the brick autoclave
under the laundry room, screams rise up chutes
while the sergeant's leg is sawed off above the long sock.

The clock is a black box with lipstick
on it: *not awake,*
I throw Bill Knott's last volume
at it... *two bogies, then, at three o'clock?*

A small Chinaman and a woman in a white dress
watch the blossoming
hand grenades like running buffalo
whose legs have gone out

under them—dead almost,
eating the sudden shifting geysers of dirt
that circling Cree ponies drift through, invisible
in the mind of a dry old woman,

all colors fading for her
like the smell of her daughter's urine—
the buffalo meat, pyrite crystals
of hashed fruit:

        goddamn *comma* Bill *comma* but
when I read you
I dream as guilty as Lincoln, at midsummer,
out in the copse yard in the cooling suburbs
of Washington.

The Hour

The linden tree lifts
in the strong summer wind. Four pigeons
are reflected in a turquoise confusion
of water and sky. One pigeon
rising above a strong swimmer's back...

the night is aghast.

Herman Melville's Book of Four Sentences

The snow fence could be seen
leaving a woman who's eating cold noodles.

It's not made of abandoned bee boxes
or, egotistically,
like a medieval famine in Japan.

Here, the Quaker whalers
are scaling a ladder
into the idealized heavens.

A ladder
made of fresh DNA of snow fence:
these pious hunters
are screaming and waving to their children:

they sigh and say *bye-bye:*
their gums
bleeding like glaciers,
like the receding hairline of acacia
                              on Mt. Sinai...

Not the Bathing Tank at Madras: A Romance

The morning's mail rises up the stairwell
with its simple breakfast; postage from Gambia
rivaling the khaki toast and jam, pomegranate
for importance both of paint
and shrinking perspective. The orchid goes
nervous in its stringy waist
for the master does not answer
Gertie's repeated knocking. Her husband

rests a wooden ladder
against the evidence of black glass
making a mask
with his large hands against the new sun,
he peers into the locked room
tapping on the window with an appropriate

rhythm that reminds him
of haying bells. He then begins his descent
wondering if with old Harold dead
will the younger master
leave him to starve
out among the rocks of a yawning heath.

His good foot, which is only middling today,
is testing the air
for a ladder rung or the untimely lawn
while he begins to fall
toward a railing of iron lilies and javelins.

The orchid on its pewter tray
screams waking old Harold
who farts so loudly
that Gertie begins to laugh and cry
from her hallway,
now greeting the unlikely Lord

who opens the door to his cool dark tank
as if it were a solemn medieval lake.

Tibet

The big dog is eating its own jowls,
is eating snow
with its blooded jowls.

By morning it is frozen solid
despite the excellent yellow beetle
from Beijing
on the mastiff's white collar.

Just for the moment
the ghost of the dog
is aroused by the ghost of a passing camel:

they are exchanging a simple *fuck-you*
on a wind
corrupted by a quick passage of goats.

Please try to explain it
to these nasty, nasty bastards.

We knew it was all shaping up like this!
Everything
everywhere is feeding.

By midnight, the snowy faded conversation
between the dog and camel
is the only thing
that really matters...

In These Streets with the Binary Trees

elegy for Neda Agha-Soltan

Yesterday, in a refusal
of evening
the griffins, wings
resting in red sand verbena,

sucked sleep from the eyes
of a motorcyclist's father
who offered boiled rice
to the men of a mathematical
ballroom...

snow falling from fur coats
into the canals
of hell as a proviso

against all weather
in a yellow pot of African
violets...

equatorial, despotic *whether you do,*
whether you don't, dead
in fact, *if you do,*

if you don't,
suppose for the moment,
which is all it takes, an envelope

is passed from one supreme calabash
to the next, in a musical
rendition now

showing
its teeth like the piano swallowed
by seawater,

actually seawater
is pouring from the tap, it's as if

the day's events have caught up with
us, the planet
involved with its own laughter
like sodium feldspar in granite.

The Volcano

The filling station is a blue can
of sardines edged with rose granite,
rope and wooden ore buckets
at the high-water nest of burning grass
in the baking mud of the paloverde.

A giant sloth limp in tractor gears, the vast
related machines of a priest's calculations,
the far river of bodies
with the drowned nun,
her back arched over a tree limb, caked
to white mud—a heavy moth between her legs
lifts across the pitching sulfur
of the approaching night.

Green fruit on a card table.
At the roadside, a small boy
gnawing on corn smiles
with efficient hunger—no one else
is alive for a hundred square miles—
the road ruptured above and below him—
the jaguar smiles back
in a white cap of ash

that is also the night:
he watches
the boy eat, he fears him
and retreats with the mice into the hot-banded night.

Cantor, Frege & Gödel:

Loosening spiders across the inert baritone
of transfictional time,
he describes the exact absence
of moment in equilibrium,

a beehive of rotating universes,
devising space like a plate
of spaghetti, white
in white sauce, a priori
arithmetic in a physical world.

The hidden language rises
to meet its own magnetism—
it is safe here
for all us rabbits. Larkspur,
lake, a gravy of lamb bone.

The sorrow in all this
is less than our objection
to old age, suffering,
and death by grasshopper.

Kurt asks how a delectable fat insect
can create a successful famine?
In the logical city their antennae, wings, and legs
are burned by the bushel as fuel.

And even the King delights in them
when first dipped in ashes and gruel.

Spirit Pond

We put our ears
to the iron grate of the ceiling.
Marge White
sat at our kitchen table
telling Ruth that William said
it was the hottest contest
that he'd lost in a lifetime
of fighting winter fires.
(Cutting

through ice, a big horse
burning down by the marsh.)
Exploding propane canisters beheading
Mr. Moore, leaving his wife
only sunburnt but stone-deaf in both ears—

her four children and a stupid pig
screamed inside the farmhouse—she couldn't
hear them, of course, but
she knew to look for it in the faces of the men—
volunteer firemen angling
away from her
with black hoses that ran to the pond:

the older sister after a tall scotch
said that the men were like fish
with great strings of shit leaving them
moving crazily to be free of it.

Mrs. Moore finally put both hands
over the young minister's ears—
his eyes flooding, she knew then
and ran into the fire looking
for her missing shoe. The minister
had been trying to return it to her—seconds later

the house collapsed
and he threw the old boot in after her; he was
angry and dismayed, her newborn

there in the arms of a newspaper man
from Bath who put the infant back
in the trembling arms of the Reverend
and then never wrote another inch of newsprint.

He became a schoolteacher in a distant village
in Massachusetts.

Le Monde

The early morning stench
of chemical shacks is heating up
at first light, walking off
into the crepe of a greening gravitational swamp
of idiot purchase,
of adamantine North Atlantic tolerance
for alligators and opossum—
in fact the blue-red sauce
the opossum bobs in
has risen with scallions, moons of garlic,
and a lizard who fell
into the pot along with a high shelf's
relics: a vulgar shaving of bone
from Jerusalem, a moody
saint's letter of complaint about gallstones,
and a young Jesuit's scalp taken twice somehow
by an old crazy Algonquin called Quiet Pierre
who turned cannibal himself
in a dark March storm, remembered
for the size of its hail, volleying thunder,
and a lightning strike that melted a small church bell
down its rope onto the floor of the scented vestibule—
close, very close
to the center of the red old city
of Montreal.

On a Plain of Jars

The water buffalo walks away
into the dark trees to the left, flypapers
on red-and-yellow stick
emerge from enormous termite nests...

like stupas seemingly milkless...
but with eyes of honey
and red lips,
with the list
of two meats and two vegetables
and that green pack of cigarettes,

please just forget us.

Desiccated Deer Akimbo in Barbed Wire

Beyond the winter of its death
it folds like a weight of rag
beyond the grasses,
beyond the other deer
who recognized through blowing snow
a struggle with metal burr
high up in cold air, finally
that single leg and groin, not quite
of hesitation, but again,
weight and its unlikely distribution
making difference
the dead.

Sunset over Decatur, Illinois

The clay fields reflect the opal of moon
back at the moon. This is how the new
hunger in the suburbs
is best understood. That
and the coyote smoke
from the old factory
that has burned down
in January thaw: the rain seemingly
bears fire into the maw
and the cold
is coming on with the sun's shyness.

This day
the shelling over Gaza
killed children
at play in their schoolhouse.

It killed a white-spotted
mouse with a red beard
and a fallen gold collar.

The sun setting over Decatur, Illinois,
seemed not to give a shit—
it didn't falter.

The Arbor

When my neighbor, who lives
in the apartment below,
opens his water tap
I feel less alone,
and I know this embarrasses you
but further,
to tell the truth,
at such moments
I often look
with interest
at a green and red packet
of sunflower seeds
that cost me, nine
years ago, $1.29.
I bought it for my wife.
The cat
with her nose behind the ragged ficus
points to the small darkening gecko
scribbling on the wall
something Islamic.
A dwarf is now crying
in my neighbor's kitchen,
he sounds swollen but golden
with malediction.
My neighbor, a celebrated logician,
has taken to calling the dwarf
Lucille.
On the table there are fossils
like cauliflower dipped in cheese.
The dwarf will not starve
and for that matter
neither will I
unless I am mistaken
deeply about the value of seeds.

II

The Salt Cedar Fires of '08

She said in the dark church kitchen
that the moon was on her
and so she put her last clean sock up inside her,
that she slept last night
in an automobile, was sober
but wouldn't be much longer,
that the fires choked her—
the smoke, she thought, was greasy
and intolerable like Phoenix itself.

The Navajo, whom she admired,
said this town
was hell at the level of seawater.
She adjusted a shoulder
and regretted once more
not being a blonde. Though she *was*
insisted the deacon. She lifted her
hem to him and smiled
like Cavafy chewing an olive.

In Iceland

                    Not that distant
from its sun
there's a fishing village, Höfn,
with a river of ghosts
proud of their stony redoubt
and blood-orange horizon,
a promenade of dead innocent
citizens of Iraq
visiting in their transmigration
and hoping to taste
the cooked eyes of sheep
with chicory coffee
and the meat of red salmon. They are
not lost—we are
it would seem. Yes, I've brought
you to this so we can pick
violets on the hillside
and be forgiven.

History

Blackman Sklar, to say it simply, had
a stand of bamboo
behind his blue pickup and garden.

Once, while the wind was entering those trees,

I suddenly saw
a great wide river alive with dead men and boys
who had just been emptied from a Greek battlefield
into the dark water. There were hundreds
of dead horses.

I was, there, in that cold river with them.

Two days earlier, I was the rich merchant returning by sea
to his three daughters in Antioch.
My oldest had a cleft lip, spoke five languages,
and was an excellent barber.

It was her I heard in the sky above me
as I was drowning. Her voice combined with water
to produce a sound
of wind
moving through Blackman Sklar's bamboo...   and

him shouting, "Jesus, man! Now where have you
gone to?"

2012

All of the crabshacks are burning,
gulls are circling
the open crates of avocados in the snow
out beyond
even the earth's gravity.

This must be the judgment. A ladder
reaching us from a nursery of suns
once spun by collisions
along the grazing edge of Sagittarius
and the Milky Way. The plate galaxies
had not been so lucky. Bill Knott,

that lovely man, who nudged Jim Wright
back from the string of leopard trout, says
a calendar is just a colander,
just an anxious hourglass—water
trading for sand,
sand trading for oil. Now, is this

the end in stone wheeling above our heads, the
great firesale
of the fat Chinese sow-dog?

Say it slowly with peace in your heart,
"I sure the fuck hope not."

The Flower Octagon of Old Manhattan

Laura said it must be a vagina of cabbage
with an army of white ants.
The postman in kneesocks
wears an aluminum-foil hat
over his long red locks.
The bats are leaving their caves
and with some haste we have discovered early evening.

Hog intestine packed
with pickled meats and the lavender heather
of this past spring are hanging
from the ceiling.

All the Sopranos
were butchered in that booth.
An eyeball rolling across the floor,
not in silence, nearly though.

It was the daughter
who put the fork in his eye—
a glass prosthesis.
He put a butter knife in her esophagus,
flooding the lungs with blood.
Most poor members of the audience,
typically and with exasperation,
adjusted the knobs on their televisions.

No one was prepared for the future trouble
in our banks. Least of all
the banks. You believe that?

Before leaving,
of course, he thought to retrieve
the eyeball. Polishing it
on his long sleeve. The pig intestine
blushing beyond belief. Electricity
leaving his hands for the streets.

The Fourth Generation of Summer

in memory of V. Aksyonov

This July, all the winged insects
and their egg sacs are wintering
in the lightness
upstairs in drying towels of a dead lioness.

The begonia snores
at the windowsill where sparrows
recite from the lost Russian's novels—the nicotine
stains on his stubby fingers
move without prejudice
against the white blinds of termites
in the rafters...   Vasily, again

all of the corpses smell of the lilacs hashed by a thunderstorm
crisscrossing the hills.
I would like a cigarette now

myself—
but old man, I did love your books
and the red and gold cloak
of nearness
you wore that last night, wet
and cold, starting
the furnace
while rising with its smoke
in fresh translation, bones
to electric bonnet.

Of the Roman Gladiator's Mad Elephant

He took spears in the neck—and when
at eye-level
the woman on the rooftop
saw blood and air
shooting equally from his nostrils
she stopped bathing
her two sons, abandoning
the sickly one
while running into the clay arches
dragging the other
by a now-broken elbow
that had fat on it like a bamboo wick.

And everything ends
in a world of symbols.

In a world of shit
for the banker's daughter who threw
a burning lamp into the elephant's
open face; blind now
he crashes through their house
killing an old woman servant in mirrors
and the banker himself.

The wind turns pages
in the old book of changes.
And everything ends
in a world of symbols.
Everything ends in a world of regret.

Untitled for Christopher Burawa

I told my friend
that hundreds are now dead
from cholera in West Africa

and he asked is that rats
or water—my grandfather
went out to his barns
in Iceland in the early dark
and if he had rats he would have placed basins
of sweet bourbon
at every third stanchion
and then from lamplight
he'd pull the unconscious rats out of straw
and into copper pails
of ammonia and water. With the yellow-gloved hand
he would drown them.

This world grows to be too terrible,
he says—I know it can't last—take the weather
by example…

The Lost Adages of Maestro Pacal

The secretary of storks
is dancing to cantina music
with an opened umbrella, its cavity
so black and vast
it seems an exhaust
of imagination
drifting across a deer herd
in western Massachusetts.

The deer are imaginary
with lice
or an application of aspirin...

a sudden snow in April morning,
in April evening, is like
the death of a local hunter
bearing the five forces
of nature away
from the gravid
toward an intelligible
bacon and cucumber sandwich.

A thermos of cold tea.

And the stars inside the umbrella
begin to turn
clockwise, freeing us
of all intended consequences, all,
that is,
but the mantle of snow
still falling across the deer
who are grazing at the edge of a marsh
quite frozen at its equator.

The Black Canal at Bruges

circa 1411

Eleanor did dream that foo fighters
were kept beside the canal
in leg irons
as sure as her husband
under the great mahogany task
of a midnight thunderstorm
that only Churchill slept through
up to his chin in a blanket of bourbon.

FDR promising his mother
they would scour the tobacco "sherbet"
from all the walls
before she returned to sleep
there in late November.

But what did the first lady
see in the reflecting pond
at the White House? A painting
that she once desired?
The end of plague years?
Or a simple broom
soaked in whitewash

that an angry crone has
thrown against a passing cart
of smelly Flemish potatoes?

The watery oculus at night
devoured her twice,

Eleanor thought. Not her
but the crone. Now substitute
the one for the other
and there is a wound. A mound.
And Winston Churchill, curse him,
snoring through it all.

An Early Morning for Tito

They wanted us to think of the pocket watch
as a sunny egg.
The importance of the minute hand survives
a folding edge of time,
a hinge of time
as when the Mesa *Tribune*
falls to my neighbor's balcony at 3 a.m.
scaring the cat more often
than me.

I quiet her by saying something
about the now confused
and celibate molecules
of the dead mouse
resting at the bottom
of Cézanne's ginger pot which is
often rescued from the cold black floor
of the China Sea,
not with the irritability
of memory
or new cheese, but to be
one of the apostles of death
and yet to write this verse
for a friend's mirror happiness.

In a World of Cows

I am afraid.

I am the near and distant grass.

                                   The raw milk
threading the let
in the tongue of the rat.

Just the tongue of the calf
in a tub of salt
on the table
where the corpse of Uncle John
was washed. He had, I am adding,
soiled his long blouse—

grandmother, like the grave itself.

A Nativity Canvas for My Daughter

July 18, 1969

Theo is still dreaming of the trees'
deposits of copper and fleece
and the rouge fleshy wings of an angel
with bad teeth
holding a torch to a wall
where the dragging automatic hand
paints us in red and ochre—
the message is simple, *come*
over, come over now,
the small wooden boats
have only the appearance of cows
climbing in the mist
while the sowers enter the fields
not quite awake
with their slings spilling seeds
for the organizing crows
in their dim seasonal disbelief—
not the usual mischief of feeding,
more a moment of grace and sudden snow.

III

Bureau Case Number LXXXVIII

The improbable physical martini
had for a boat
a rubber lotus of a thousand petals
in a cooling tub
with a black cake of Lava soap
in a woman's red wig of burnt wool.

J.

Julius Oppenheimer is now cleansed,
if not in history, then
here, simply hiccuping, worrying

over an increase in equine encephalitis
in the hills of New Mexico
while his cupcake rides a fresh bidet
in the suburbs of ancient Crete.

The buffalo rug
beside the tub is rising
to devour him...
dear dark oriole, ici—

well, this girl sings R&B
the way children eat snow,
allowing it to float into the open mouth,
crocodile,

ici repose...

The Protestant Rye

for Kaya

It was a dark rainy day with angels
eating yellow soup
with a bread like large cellular mushrooms—
the oldest of them had white splinters
in her elbows. A leopard
snoring on the rug behind her
could be heard clearly
through the stone walls
by whole enclaves of field mice
undisturbed by the loud
sinus of cats—
the silence of leopards
in large referenda of rain
on the other hand
woke even their dead ancestors, punished
often by angels for carrying disease
and merriment to children.
Mostly the young children of socialists
eating black horse chestnuts
in one wet southern fjord
of Iceland where the mothers converted
again to Roman Catholicism
in a wind bearing fish and bread
to those of them not wholly barren with wisdom.

The Canvas Boat

A clean fog off slowly boiling macaroni,
a palette stone with ochre and rouge—
long brushes like dead muskrats
and a row of wild onions
with knuckles of garlic
obviating the solitary Dutch painter's
whistling while crushing azure,
crushing azure—everyone is dead
so this is the place to do this—
his blouse on fire with moon.

The Grazing Higgs Bison

for Mila

The snow falling around them
isn't mysterious, more
the shame—the collision
between patterns in ice
falling from atmospheres
and vermin in the coat of bison
grazing in landscape
isn't mysterious to the religious
in a hallway of magnets,
is indifferent to a materialism
imagined like theories
about some distant lamp burning in the Hyades.

The inert solids
of hair and clay are dedicated
to airs around Batavia, are envied
like tennis players
drinking lemonade in shade
while donkeys bray across fields outside Jerusalem.
It's slim evidence
of anything but bison
volleying in a world of fleas
that are herding like bison
over a dark level plain—

and here's the difference
between the farmer and the egg. The egg
came first, all immaculate idea
with hot water being poured
up and down its legs
so it would appear
there on the horizon above the lake
where two tall girls

have just water-skied
naked past their Principal's autumn manse,

his appropriate wife
who teaches physics to the children
now facedown
in the cottage cheese... gone
entirely faint in her fresh paint.

Untitled

The gentle cuckold Warren Harding
was not buried
with his brass tuba
though we all go to the grave
with various musical viscera,
at least that idea of it, of stomach,
before the undertakers
undertake the great
vacuums of space
and a confused heart—the funeral train back
from Alaska
put whole villages of children
up in the trees
to spy on their betters
rotting and farting
at the level of the displaced crows
who are
happy at the final passing of a great man,
his golden locomotive, and black sleepers
one after another to a rusting horizon.

In the Night Dulse of White Breakers a Falstaff Drops His Pike.

September 22, 2011

The moon shifts thrice in fast clouds.
He severs the Spaniard's fat arm
while the sea lifts
both men's skirts
and large birds repeat a melancholy relief.

In short they're both fucked. In good
and sudden company. A dagger leaving
the other's neck, a red
froth of oxygen at the mouth
like sea bass fertilizing rocks.

Linen sail burning far to the north.

The Spaniard's nose falls off. The birds
do their thing. Israeli kings
dead in the fog sing with ears
sealed with wax and bread.

The ship's burning far off—
what we foolishly thought...

Pastoral

Moose standing in sacerdotal soapberries
while the Sox are drifting
out of the radio's amber vacuum
across a methane pond
to the young mother from Bangor
who is bathing in a cloud of mosquitoes
cut with bats
and the night's first stars—

She is remembering her
dead aunt's nosebleed
on the farm, how the March lamb
in her arms
became serious in the simple paint
of it and pardoned them

without their knowing it—
their startled laughter
lifting a spilling moon into the elm

vividly gone.

Stockbridge Reservation

There's sickness in the boats,
the trees clearing the sky
of an easy hoax of lightning
and ground smoke.
i remember the pilgrim women
playing ball in a beach of raw sugar, crows
around the perimeter
and the gymnasts
like swollen giotto angels falling
from their devices
at some depth of water
we watch a black sow
admiring old women
doing their wash
in silver quake water...

the iridium, mercury thumb
back on the horizon—
how many gorges women
in swimming costumes
hanging their wash in the trees,
the daughters of protestant carpenters
all with morning sickness.
In fact, there's sickness in the boats...
Jonathan Edwards has wrapped
his left hand in blue corn shuck,
anointing a spotted Indian dog
with a terrible squirrel
in its mouth; the mystic Edwards
was bitten first by the squirrel twice
and then by the squalid dog, the red squirrel
now flying in the trees,
its chatter a recognizable sermon
distracting to the daughter's young baby,
christened that morning Aaron Burr, who bears
his grandfather's fresh blood

on his flat forehead
into a new world
not nearly savage enough
for any of us.

Sasquatch

I am not a costume
stuffed with the organs of deer
and possum—a bucket
of huckleberries from the distant meadows.
They shot me
twice in the stomach
with dimes. The truck dragging
me for miles along
the creek. Ideas
die hard is what
the car salesman said to my wife
after cleaning his boots and his knife.

Puke

John Law is eating hot purple beets
in the poorhouse
in a dark corner of Alsace-Lorraine
where the lamps weaken
while he suffers a vision of complexity,
of paper money falling
upon prepositions, no, rats,
upon rats
swimming in the long canal
of next winter's early rains.

John Law is a membrane
of least fact—the idea of paper money
is Chinese, just,
as animal crackers are Sumerian and puke
to most dogs
is a late least fact of appetite
all over again—

it is strange
that the financing of the American Revolution
and John Law's printing machines
led to the bankruptcy
of the entire French nation
and hundreds, perhaps thousands,
of headless aristocrats
as if money were a kind of contingency
like rain.

Stringy Goats of Gold Nuclei Evaporate Before My Eyes

The grim whole numbers are hiding
just beyond the bleak horizon—
here we slow to picnic
in ejaculate heat death, the quanta
of assassins
like so many seedless watermelon
squatting on the dictator's trestle table.

The flatlanders'
description of degrees of imagination
will never share a very dry martini
with the intolerant rosy holograms
who count the burning candles
on their mother's layered cake.

As I understand their point of view—
abstract,
masturbatory, and edged
with blue chiffon chits of goo...

gesundheit, in triplicate, is their reply...

and translates into *boo...*

Again the Twentieth-Century Realism

The wolf looks up with its bloody mouth
to a hundred reindeer
wearing snowshoes—famine
beyond the lake did this to them
like a parenthesis ripening
in graded school to the exclusion
of burning miner's-candles
and the black flags of kerosene
they were soaking in—

the shooter above the woods
reads the poetry of Tsvetaeva,
her prose, too, wiping tears
not from his eyes
but from full lips, a mustache
of eyelash frozen there
with green ponds of mucus
and a small fox leaping
at a crow that speaks
the parenthesis of late winter
and flies farther north
between equal blue columns of octane and disgust.

The Siege of Horizons

circa 1968

Christmas night in Vicksburg—the family
is at the door with carolers—
the one-eyed cat
has dragged the small venison roast
past a heat death and flatness
with curvature
to cellar stairs
where the mud crawlspace is telling
this story of a poor observable universe.

The cat, who is not allowed out of doors,
nevertheless
presented the mistress once
with a dead cottonmouth
and also, years later,
a thirty-pound seagull
with thread-hatching of tail feathers
like patched sail.

The parlor's baritone could not
have predicted this even against
some prolonged happiness
that is and isn't a confinement.

Yet, hunger is as important as measles—
munitions wagons
boiling up along the river.

The Magnesia Caesar

I killed the big wharf rat
with the rack of my abacus,
many red numeral beads
appeared in the rue and poppy spray—
I took the paper poppy of trade,
I took the opportunity
to inventory missing sacks of grain
for poor towns in Palestine,
for the messengers of the nearer towers
of rubies and glass—
those future cities, little Miza and Puy.
Awk, but

I'm haunted by the illustrated houses
of these magnificent Christians—
the faces even of their old women;
sure they're a pain in the ass
but the colors
of their sunsets behind skull hills
are an actual visitation of the future...
This is not my sickness
flaring, *thank you very much.* Dearie,
put the wine there. I am
shaking inside this morning. Agreed,
their sunsets
cannot be forgiven by me.

Their blood is not everywhere.

IV

A New Moon

I will not see it.

Jubilee of Surprising Agreement

The voice starts in the trees.
A colored cloud from the Bering Sea
in arc minutes over the train depot
says: *It will never see it.*

Cantors with green eyes
and solid gold teeth
carrying fans of black palm
sing: *We have not wanted to see it.*

The new moon draws
threads through their many hearts
until the streetwalker, Mademoiselle Poincaré,
turns to the Cantors
showing an arbitrary esteem
like beaded urns of raw milk and
it's her voice rising in the trees
into a single speech,

I will not see it.
It will not see me.

The smaller of her two breasts now
winks in photoelectric spontaneity
like a Russian villain in a silent movie
and the children in the grandstand
sing *jubilee...*

The Song of the Strangelet

The sailors are proper envoys
to a picnic table, hard-
boiled eggs
rotating in fields of salt—
chrysanthemum petals
like a discharge in the trees
and the abduction
occurs in the early evening,
whole stadia of magnets
showing teeth. Two Swiss
playing basketball
with rifles and cigarettes.
The algorithm in an open field
abducted by a romance of wheelbarrows—
science like all superstition
fondles the grim ignorance
that is chance, chance
of course is the teakettle
waking father by the fire
that could be a particle accelerator
liberating its first ghost,
a machinist extrovert
standing at the end
of a lensing
twelve thousand galaxies in width—
he waves at the youngest of the sailors
who shows
him the middling digit of proverb's three,
our very ether
ruptured by it. Who could
eat at Joe's
              after this?

Plaquemines Parish

Parsifal, walking through a train wreck
in East Los Angeles.
In one burning car
the watercolorist's
fox is sunken in snow—
a Japanese woman darkly combing
her lover's mustache. Advertisements
for chewing gum
above the policeman pinned by
the awning of a cattle car. That night's hurricane,
the size of the gulf, says,
"What of it?"
I throw cards
with the dead,
who answer, "The birds have
stopped singing,
the skyline is yellowing." Parsifal
is taking tickets for his trouble.

The Boxcars of Mars

Two green arms in eggshell light
climb beyond darkening trees
to the snow line
and a miracle of sleeves—adamantine
waters dividing deer
that stream past the old priests
who are boiling tubs of tea.

Clouds banking at the mountains
descend into fir trees and night fog.
The deer slow and make applause
while eating snow. The last deliberate
moon spits at the old priests,
who spit back...

The deer are urinating on the corpse
who ate a small sack of gold
and his family knows to bring him
back home by long rail.
They'll salt him down at the depot
and finally open him
with the same shovel brought for the burial.

Did this happen deep in the past somewhere
or in the near future.

The priests are not Shinto.

Pontius Pilate

The figs at supper were mealy. Just
as they were in her dream. It is
what she said by way
of excusing her favorite servant. A Thracian
who lost two fingers
to Herod's cousin.

I despise these people
for what they would do with horses alone.
In my wife's dream there is a man
with heavy eyelashes and long soft hands
and he reminds her of her dead brother
martyred with a mouth full of fire ants.
Like smoke almost
she says they reach my hair.
And, naturally,
the figs have turned to meal.

I tell her she'll forget her brother,
that time heals
even the big bowl of vinegar
in its alabaster closet.

She says the sudden humidity has made
a face across the lavatory walls
and that our soldiers are talking about it
at their fires. *The voices are
full of fear.* About this

she is right.

Also, I'll interject, there are fat
yellow striped worms in our rice. The Thracian
called them mule maggots.
                    I dread each night.

The Early Evening Phenomena of Winter Sabbath

The man who carried the snow awl
out the far monastery wall
was charged with the full measure
of three nights' accumulation—
was charged, of course, the certain thought
that this snowfall was historical
across centuries...

The old man was our cook and his apron
was stained with black tea and red roots.

He had already accomplished his task
while seated in the choir loft
but this gift for remote experience
brought nosebleeds and mild seizures,
which upset the abbot
who thought all such afflictions
were attractive to demons, so
the cook bled from the pine trough
to the cobbler's closet
where the ancient snow awl
rested in cedar chips with frankincense.

When the old man stepped out
onto the leviathan snows he was,
as he had seen an hour before,
swallowed utterly by them;
his body, discovered in late spring, was
fresh but frowning.

The abbot said: Let this be a lesson
to you all
that even righteous acts of heroic laziness
are not forgiven
by our Creator who is
obverse and absolute like the leg bone

of a goose carved into music
that is issuing from a flute.

The Sabotage of Arks

for Wallace

The ghosts of bulls
fly in through the window, a layering
of pond water and plumlike skin—
babies in China are turning this color
from stones in their milk, turning
to the testimony of their mothers
gone mad

with screams of an unabashed night
of suffering.
And the baker crosses the street
with his red and yellow accordion
loosed in his arms
to symbolize that your suicide
is meaningless to the Beijing postal clerk
with ice-cold feet and a broken arm.

The Exeter Messenger Aboard the RMS *Lusitania*

Actually, it might have been
the *Ferdinand Magellan*—
the waist of subversion
and all those
brightly dimming villains
versus the mood
of expiration
and the simple screw peeling
the potato for the turtle soup.
The hundred-year-old
meat softening in purple wine
under the cook's hammer
that ripples in a cold salty air
of a vacant steerage
with ten giant turtles
who'll swim
away from this cursed vessel.
A calliope of turtles
bobbing in the North Atlantic
sharing their rote discourse
on humanity—
their prehistoric horse heads
jabbering over
the officers' starched shirts—
remnant with water—
these old underestimated
creatures
in a short-legged laughter
about what a crew
of pitiless motherfuckers
we were, all the rats
drowning, too.

Landmine: Field of Copper Wings

We are the swimmers, with legs and arms.

We sleep beside the river
and dream of the Joshua tree...

In the mountains of Afghanistan

there are swarming bees
painted across the smokehouse door
so we will remember

the soft meaty comb, the shelf
of gore.

The Ceremony

The wedding veils are oppressing them,
are in the trees singing
like yellow frogs back from the river—
the cows, too, are
just returned from the river
and they are singing loudly
to the frogs a dull repo
of magistrate's vows, a blue-haired
shaman descends from the clouds saying
Lucky Strikes means fine tobacco,
golly gee...

it's the nicotine in the insecticide
that's killing the bee larvae,
they are the long sleeper—
human beings
are climbing into the trees
to steal the veils,
accidentally they are pollinating
the pear orchards. The paper hives
are burning.
It's a good time to be alive
and well in Sacramento. That is,
before the floods and the volcano.

The Dead Madrigal Bears of Afghanistan

for Paul Cook

They wear the clever hats
of the Dog Star, of wehrmacht palettes,
not, mind you,
the German officers, but the bears
who are the visitors!

A blue light around their collars
and gold foil for long sleeves.
They *are* giant, they do bleed
the cold fat of rationed Spam.
They read Eckhart to their children—the sermon
on being subtracted from stone.
They have lost all tolerance

for clear-cutting in the Amazon,
so they will invade soon—the celebrated
unbuttoning of strangelets in mino-railings,
in delayed proton escort,
and the stargate will activate like a Swiss franc.
So much for the scribes of cholera, rice
shortages, and the blue pomegranate
with a white worm in it.

They have been hunted into sleep
where the clean-lifts
of their planet remain pinstripe
behind a dark vacant lensing.
They will carry banners that say:

THE SECRET POLICE CAN KISS MY ASS. This would
be unpleasant,
unpleasant at best with bears,

or aliens reflecting off the trapezium of Orion.

They do wash in buckets
where the moon reflects a calculus
full stop. Blessed.
But blessed against the new terror.
And the very old bearded cigars
of our planet.

Tiresias in an Arcturus Springtime

for Hayden Carruth

The fields of Thebes were not recognizable
to him. Though
they were clearly seeded with yellowing teeth.
There were dimensions of song here
like sacks hanging from whitened trees.
The back gate of the city was blind
by day.

The ghosts in the streets were, he thought,
at play. There were women near?
But he couldn't say
even that the copulating snakes
were all eights.

Frogs walked out of the pond, the very spangle
of Arcturus in their eyes. The coins
in their hands made of a children's clay.
When it began to rain the frogs
began to cry:

Tiresias, you are a blind decoy
for the mother of us all,
the walls of Thebes
are made of our coins.
Your loins
are just some poor wager at best.

Tiresias, you have seen
all this.
It is not your death.
But a momentary indiscretion.
A last breath
you both lost and kept.

Not Noon, 1904

for Meghan L. Martin

I

Poincaré sits in the turning dark
of the stairwell
folded in a thin nightshirt
eating a dry husk of carp, mostly
all huge brass head, eyes
distraught,
with declining bones like a harp.

An influenza is in the suburbs.
The lamps
will be sputtering
with a soloist birdsong
that separates his thoughts. Bells

like "little grisha" in low declensions—
the white loins of the leopard
in flight through the windows
of the lyceum
washed with vinegar and small sunfish.

The bell rope falling
from the night sky is the last secret—that,
and his perspective of the first stanza
as a composition
in six dimensions, the uncommon
equilibrium.

2

The zebra stands in the back
of the beer truck
eating straw off blocks of ice...
the zebra has pollywogs
on it like lice, field
lines of wiggly sentience
and the pink mice insisting, cropside,
of a plague outside Marseille
and Nice.

3

The beer truck drives into the dusk.
The untroubled potato fields
egging on a soloist bird,
at evening; it sings
of the *überframes* and the long
long bell rope at dawn.
Grisha, common
monotony of enigma is what's wrong.
It's grisha who now mourns.

The Gate

You will not see it.

Notes

"Desert Carousel: Missiles and Instructions" is dedicated to the memory of Kenneth T. Salls.

"Behind the Old Soldiers' Hospital" is for Meghan.

"Le Monde" is for Brian Young.

"Desiccated Deer Akimbo in Barbed Wire" is after the photograph by Michael Berman and was a presentation piece at his Lannan exhibit in Santa Fe in the winter of 2008.

"In Iceland" is for Christopher Burawa.

"2012" is for Doug and Elizabyth.

"Stockbridge Reservation" is dedicated to the memory of the poet Ai.

"The Ceremony" is for Laura Johnson.

Norman Dubie was born in Barre, Vermont, in April 1945. His poems have appeared in many magazines, including *The American Poetry Review, Gulf Coast, The Paris Review, The New Yorker, Poetry, Crazyhorse,* and *Field.* He has won the Bess Hokin Award of the Modern Poetry Association and fellowships from the Ingram Merrill Foundation, the John Simon Guggenheim Memorial Foundation, and the National Endowment for the Arts. Mr. Dubie won the PEN USA prize for best poetry collection in 2001. He has recently published a book-length futuristic work, *The Spirit Tablets at Goa Lake,* online with *Blackbird.* He lives in Tempe, Arizona, with the cat Fast-Eddie-Smoky-Chokyi-Lodrö, and teaches at Arizona State University.

Since 1972, Copper Canyon Press has fostered the work of emerging, established, and world-renowned poets for an expanding audience. The Press thrives with the generous patronage of readers, writers, booksellers, librarians, teachers, students, and funders — everyone who shares the belief that poetry is vital to language and living.

Copper Canyon Press gratefully acknowledges board member

JIM WICKWIRE

for his many years of service to poetry and independent publishing.

Lannan

NATIONAL
ENDOWMENT
FOR THE ARTS

WASHINGTON STATE
ARTS COMMISSION

Major support has been provided by:

Amazon.com

Anonymous

Beroz Ferrell & The Point, LLC

Golden Lasso, LLC

Gull Industries, Inc.
on behalf of William and Ruth True

Lannan Foundation

Rhoady and Jeanne Marie Lee

National Endowment for the Arts

Cynthia Lovelace Sears and Frank Buxton

Washington State Arts Commission

Charles and Barbara Wright

*To learn more about underwriting
Copper Canyon Press titles, please call
360-385-4925 x103*

The poems have been typeset in Sabon, an old-style serif typeface designed by the German-born typographer and designer Jan Tschichold (1902–1974) in the period 1964–1967. Headings are set in Requiem, an old-style serif typeface designed by Jonathan Hoefler in 1992 for *Travel & Leisure* magazine. Book design and composition by Phil Kovacevich. Printed on archival-quality paper at McNaughton & Gunn, Inc.